'Twas a Golf Cart for Christmas

for

Christmas

Haley Christmas

Bye Bye II

Jeryl Christmas

Illustrated by Kristine Demetrio

This book belongs to

_____

Foreword

Because of hypotonic cerebral palsy, Haley Christmas never could talk, run, or play like others her age, but she could drive a golf cart! That is, until hers was stolen from her yard on November 4, 2009. Even though her cart was never recovered, she now drives a shiny, stylish blue one thanks to Andrew Dys, a columnist for The Herald, who told her story, along with WBTV, WCNC, and CN2. Haley's story touched hearts, resulting in generous donations given by the community and Founders Federal Credit Union. One very special person whose heart was touched was Andy Clabough, owner of Andy's Used Golf Carts, who built her a new one with the money donated. Haley cannot say "golf cart," so she calls her treasured ride her "Bye Bye." Now, thanks to the goodwill of others, she can resume riding on her track around her home waving to all who drive by.

To see Haley getting her new cart, go to the following link:

https://youtu.be/WCb97MAu-Tk

'Twas the home of Miss Christmas when in her backyard

A golf cart was stolen while no one stood guard.

The crime was reported—they gave every fact

In hopes that her "Bye Bye" soon would be back.

Miss Haley went sadly to sleep in her bed

While visions of golf carts danced in her head.

Then money was given through lots of goodwill

To lovingly help Haley's broken heart heal.

When, what to her wondering eyes should appear

But a personalized cart made by someone who's dear.

Andy put in new headlights, a radio, and bell.

She knew in a moment the story they'd tell

Of the love and the kindness from people and friends

How goodness won out and the message that sends.

She wanted to thank all the folks who took part

In touching her life and blessing her heart.

To Andy and all the community aid:

You cannot imagine the difference you've made

You're tops on her list—you're tops in her heart

She'll dash away, dash away driving her cart.

She's tingly inside from her head to her feet

A permanent smile on her face she will keep

With Gram in the front and Gramps on the back

She's ready to ride on her well-traveled track.

Her eyes how they twinkle—her face is so merry

She smiles for the camera and waves to Aunt Sherry

Taking pictures galore to remember the day

When Christmas came early in a wonderful way.

With a bow on the front of her blue "Bye Bye II,"

Chrome hubcaps and decals and mirrors brand new,

She's playing a song for the people to hear

Called "It's the Most Wonderful Time of the Year."

She can't say the words, but they all know her heart

She loves all the people who bought her new cart.

Her joy was contagious since all got to see

Her story retold in the news on TV.

CHRISTMAS COMES EARLY! NEWS

Mayor Echols saw Haley—a phone call he made

He asked her to be in the Christmas parade

Of course she accepted, excited was she,

What a wonderful evening it turned out to be!

She sprang to her cart—to the crowd she was waving

And away she did ride—these memories saving

And they know all is well as she goes out of sight

Haley Christmas signs, "Thank you," to all on this night.

The End